My first book of
Wonderful
WHEELS

A wheel is round like an `O'.
Look at the wheels around this picture.

Wheels go round and round.
This makes things easier to push,
and pull.

These children are having great fun with wheels.

Here are some wheels for babies. They make prams and buggies easy to push.

Here is a wonderful toy with lots of wheels.

Can you count them?

Pedal cart

BMX bike

Trike

Tractor and trailer

Do you have any toys like this?

Police pedal car

Tractor and bucket

Remote control truck

How many wheels can you count?
Don't forget the steering wheels.

1 My bike has one wheel.
It is very hard to stay on!

2 My bike has two wheels.
I can ride fast.

3 My bike has three wheels.
It is very easy to ride.

But my bike is a motorbike.
It is very fast...and very noisy!

This is a very old car.

This is a very new car.

This is a racing car.

This is a car transporter,
it delivers new cars
to garages.

Taxi!

This car can go over rough country.

These wheels bring us things we like.

The drivers are having to change a wheel...

Can you tell which wheel goes where?

Look at the huge wheels on these trucks.

Earth moving truck

Four wheel drive

Low loader

Do you have any toy trucks like these?

Tipper truck

Wheels take us from place to place.

This is an old steam train.

This is a new electric train.

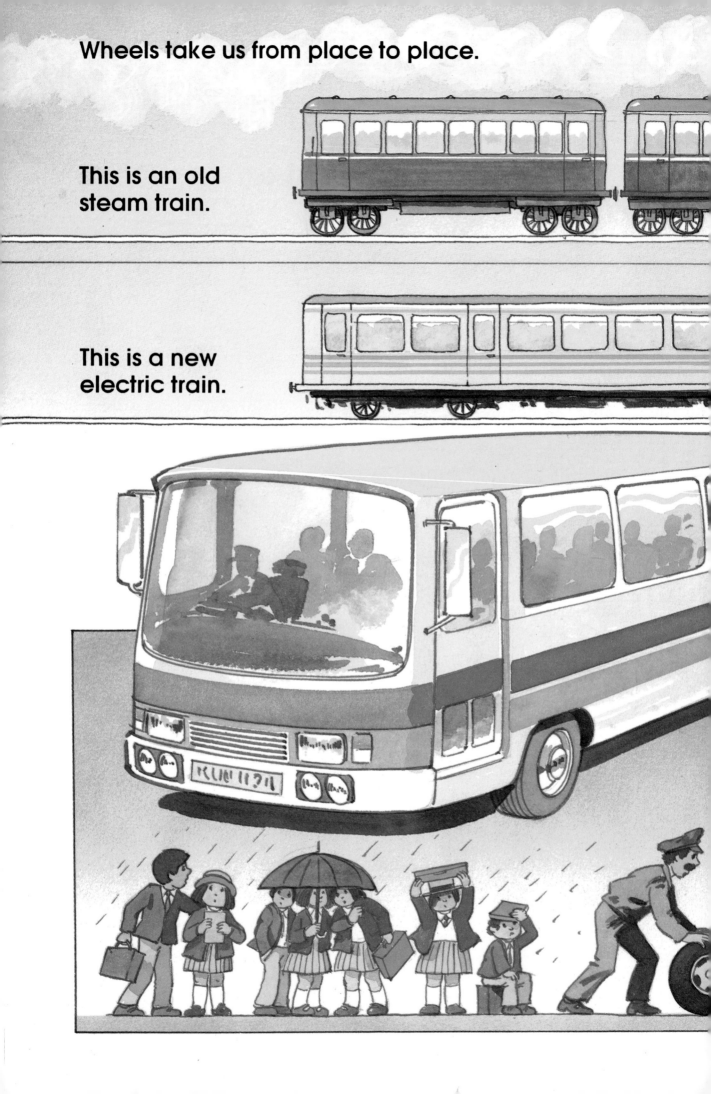

Lots of people can travel in a train or a coach.

This coach is taking people on holiday.

Oh dear, the school bus has a flat tyre, but the driver has a spare.

SCHOOL BUS

These wheels bring us help when we are in trouble or danger.

The ambulance takes people to hospital.

The motorcycle policeman
can go very fast to where
he is needed.

Here is the fire engine.
The fire will soon be put out.